GREETINGS FROM SEATTLE

L. Spencer Humphrey

THUNDER BAY
P·R·E·S·S
San Diego, California

Finding "New York Pretty Soon"

The Emerald City that rises from the Ring of Fire

The Ring of Fire is an arc that stretches along the eastern edge of Asia up through Alaska's Aleutian Islands and down along the western coast of the Americas. The area where Seattle is located is one hot spot along this ring of tectonic movement, seismic and volcanic activity. The volcanoes Mount Rainier and Mount St. Helens tower over Seattle and they, along with frequent earthquakes in the area, are vigilant reminders of the topography of this special place. But the Ring of Fire has given the area many of its greatest gifts. From the mountains themselves, to the stunning islands and natural vistas, the place that became Seattle has been luring people for many thousands of years.

Above: This image shows Captain George Vancouver's ship caught on rocks in the Sound. It is being watched over by canoes full of curious Kwakiuti people.

The first people arrived across the Bering Strait about 11,000 years ago. Their main food source was the abundant waters teaming with shellfish, cod, and salmon. In addition to the Duwamish people, who are the primary native peoples of the area today, these tribes also included the Snoqualmie, the Chinook, and the Suquamish peoples.

In 1792 a British sea captain, George Vancouver, arrived. That same year the American explorer Captain Robert Gray also got to the mouth of the Columbia River. These white men were mainly interested in the area for its abundance of beavers and otters whose pelts were highly prized in trading with Asia and Europe. Though they found the place, they went further north to Canada to set up permanent trading posts.

Between the early 1840's and 1860, as many as 53,000 settlers migrated along the

Right: Though known as "Chief Seattle," in fact the native peoples of the area had no hereditary chiefs.

Oregon Trail to the area south of Seattle. The Brits and Yanks disputed the territory between Canada and Oregon. In 1846 the two sides agreed to the present U.S./Canada border.

In 1851 the New Yorkers Arthur and David Denny led a group of settlers to Puget Sound, eventually laying claim to Alki Point in what is now West Seattle. Believing they were the founding fathers of a great city of the future, they called their camp Alki–New York: the word Alki is Chinook for "pretty soon." However, after the first rough winter, the settlement moved leeward to what is now Seattle.

Chief Seattle, the beloved leader of the Duwamish people at the time of Denny's arrival, urged his people to coexist in peace with the newcomers. Other tribes had no such welcoming feelings and hostilities grew. In 1854 the United States made a treaty granting $150,000 of goods and 2,600 acres of land to the native peoples as a reservation in return for their leaving the 2 million acres of the rest of western Washington. This created both distrust and anger that erupted in conflict in 1855. Chief Seattle and his Duwamish people were moved to the Port Madison Reservation in 1856. The settlers rewarded his peaceful nature by naming the city after him.

Following a contest in 1981, Seattle was officially nicknamed the "Emerald City"— a reference to the area's lush evergreen forests.

Below: In 1980 Mount Saint Helen erupted dramatically, causing death and damage, and covering much of the region with volcanic ash.

Getting Out of Town

Adventures and sights of the great Northwest

Above: A postcard of the lovely mountain in peaceful times

Look up! When the "mountain is out" (as Seattleites say referring to their grey weather), Mount Rainier seems to beckon with its grandeur and beauty. Mount Rainier National Park, actually about 90 miles out of town, offers more than 200,000 acres of views year-round, trails along glaciers and beside lakes, and stunning wild flower–laden meadows in summer. Rainier is the highest of the Cascade Mountains; the dormant volcano reaches 14,410 feet.

The Olympic Mountains are across the bay in Olympic National Park to the west. Getting there is half the fun as you take the Bainbridge Island Ferry across the sound to the Olympic Peninsula. The island ferries are like mini-cruises offering beautiful voyages and views back to the Emerald City and the mountains beyond. Once you arrive, outdoor sports, camping, hiking, and visiting the area's two hot springs make being in Olympic

Left: Imagine a kayak here in Sucia Island State Park Sandstone Shoreline in the San Juan Islands.

Below: Several pods of whales are often visible off the San Juan Islands.

National Park a memorable adventure.

Maybe you'll go to the San Juan Islands to go whale watching. Communities of whales, particularly orcas, who live in the waters off Vancouver Island and British Columbia, are often spotted on the west coast of San Juan Island. Or maybe you will seek history at the San Juan Island National Historical Park. You might pick up some yarn at the shop at Shepherd's Croft or tour the lavender fields at Pelindaba Lavender Farm. Of course, there are also bike and sea kayak tours to take.

On Blake Island, visit Tillicum Village where Native Americans continue to ply their traditional trades and crafts. It's an authentic and functioning village you can access only by boat. The islands off Seattle are beautiful, peaceful, and filled with adventures year-round.

Ready to drive a bit? Visit nearby Tacoma to see the Museum of Glass, home of world-famous glass artist Dale Chihuly's amazing Bridge of Glass. Or go a bit further south to Portland, Oregon, for some wine tasting, great local food, and, in season, the acclaimed roses.

Right: One of Dale Chihuly's Crystal Towers on the Bridge of Glass

Below right: At the entry to Tillicum Village visitors are met by an imposing totem pole.

Below: Mount Rainier National Park is full of wild blooms in the spring.

The World's Fair

Putting Seattle on everyone's map

Quick. What's the very first thing you imagine when you think of Seattle? The Space Needle, right? Many cities have iconic structures: the Hollywood sign, the Eiffel Tower, the Empire State Building, Big Ben. For Seattle, the most impressive and memorable image will likely be this remnant of the great 1962 Seattle World's Fair.

For six months during the spring, summer, and early fall of 1962, the eyes of the world were on Seattle. The Century 21 Exposition, as the 1962 Seattle World's Fair was actually called, drew as many as 10 million visitors, including Prince Philip of England, and celebrities including John Wayne, Walt Disney, Carol Channing, and Lassie to the city. There was even a movie shot at the Fair: the Elvis Presley film, *It Happened at the World's Fair,* started shooting as soon as school was back in session, in an effort to keep the screaming teenagers at bay.

But it wasn't the first time Seattle played host to a large international event. In fact, the city fathers had originally thought

Left: A poster featuring an illustration of the iconic tower

to host a World's Fair in honor of the fiftieth anniversary of the 1909 Alaska-Yukon-Pacific Exposition held in Seattle to commemorate the first Klondike gold shipment of 1897. So, the World's Fair Commission was launched in 1955. A year later the Civic Center bond easily passed, raising $7.5 million. That amount was matched by the state Legislature and the preparations for the fair began in earnest.

Seventy-four acres of what is now called the Seattle Center were acquired and leveled to make way for the iconic structures of the Space Needle and the Alweg monorail. They are among the few structures from the fair that remain standing. One other famous building that dates from the fair is the former Science Pavilion, now called the Pacific Science Center.

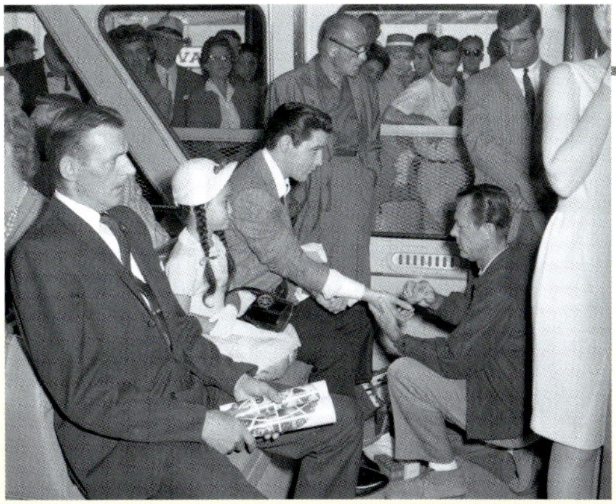

Above: This postcard shows an allegorical painting entitled *Alaska-Yukon-Pacific*, created in 1908 by the painter C.A. Holland.

Top right: Celebrities, like Elvis Presley, flocked to the fair. The futuristic auto designs featured at the World's Fair look like movie props today.

Right: The monorail takes folks around important parts of town to this day.

Left: The view of the Space Needle is almost as beautiful as the view from it.

Rain, Rain, Go Away

Outdoor living in a cold, wet city

For people who live in a place with such notoriously inclement weather, the citizens of Seattle are almost equally well known for their vigor and love of the outdoors. And there are many, many ways and places to exercise those proclivities in and around town.

Feel like a climb? Head out to the Mount Rainier National Park and you can hike up the mountain or out to the glacier's edge. Try it on horseback, if you like. There is a phenomenal two-hour ride up the mountain that lets the horses do the work while the riders enjoy the stunning views and the peace of communing with nature. Of course, you can choose to camp in this park or in the rain forest in Olympic National Park out on the Olympic peninsula. This park has several ecosystems to explore, from beaches to the alpine scenery of the mountains. Campsites abound, as do opportunities for kayaking, fishing, and communing with the wealth of wildlife in the park.

You can also spend a day at the site of the most famous contemporary volcanic

eruption in the United States—Mount St. Helens—which is now designated as a national monument.

But Seattleites don't need to travel out of the city for great outdoor experiences. From Discovery Park in the northwestern part of town, with its beaches and breathtaking views of Puget Sound, the Cascades and the Olympic ranges, to Alki Beach on the south side of Eliot Bay, there are parks that offer opportunities for walking, jogging, biking, and beaching all over town.

Want gardens? The Woodland Park Zoo and Rose Garden beckon visitors of all ages and the Botanical Garden in Bellevue is world-renowned.

Feel like fishing? There are charters and guides for all types of fishing in the area. You can cast off the Eliot Bay Fishing Pier or at Waterfront Park. And there is world-class fly-fishing in many local mountain creeks, and rivers, such as the Snoqualmie and the Yakima.

Left: The snow-covered peak of Mt. Rainier is a majestic sight.

Right: There are water sports for everyone here. White-water rafting is for thrill seekers and an afternoon in a kayak for a gentler way to commune with nature.

Below: Peaceful mountain streams tumble down the side of Mt. Rainier. For a more energetic mountain excursion, try climbing along the Skykomish River on Mt. Baker-Snoqualmie National Forest.

The Play's the Thing

Seattle's lively life in the theatre

In addition to all the outdoor activities, beer, and coffee Seattleites are known to enjoy, they also support several independent and vital theaters and theater companies.

Seattle Repertory Theatre may be the most famous of the lot. The Rep, as it is known, has been producing award-winning plays since its founding in 1963. It is one of the most well-known regional theaters in America and regularly produces both classic plays and Broadway touring companies on its three stages. In 1990 the Rep won the prestigious Tony Award for Outstanding Regional Theatre.

The Intiman Theatre, founded in 1972, took over the Play House, originally built for the 1962 World's Fair. In 2006 the Intiman also won the Regional Theater Tony Award in recognition of its excellence. More recently, the theater had to close for a time during its 2011 season due to financial exigencies, but has announced a new artistic director and will be opening for a 2012 season refurbished and refreshed.

ACT – A Contemporary Theatre is another beloved Seattle playhouse. With eight floors and multiple stages and spaces, ACT presents a wide array of contemporary performance, including site-specific pieces, conventional theater, performance art, cabaret, musicals, dance, and experimental theater. ACT also offers a Young Playwrights Program serving 300 Seattle-area schools, and each March it showcases some of the best of their plays in the annual Young Playwrights Festival.

Left: Located near the Space Needle, the Rep is notable for it's striking architecture.

At the Seattle Playwrights Collective, new plays are workshopped and produced in a series of First Look Readings, as well as the annual Page to Stage Short Play Festival.

The elegant, historic Moore Theatre, built in 1907, is the oldest remaining theater in town. Originally a vaudeville house, during the 1920s and 30s it hosted such stars as Sarah Bernhardt, Lily Langtry, and the Barrymores. The theater became a National Historic Place in the mid 1970s and most recently has become an active venue for events such as pageants, alternative music, and theater as well as dance.

The Fifth Avenue Theatre is another former vaudeville palace that is known as a "testing ground" for Broadway musicals.

The Benaroya Hall, home of the Seattle Symphony, is a stunning space notable for its amazing Chihuly chandeliers.

And there is something for the youngsters too. Seattle Children's Theatre was founded in 1975 and occupies a state-of-the-art facility with stages, and technical and classroom spaces in Seattle Center. And there are also plays and educational programs at the Northwest Puppet Center.

Top right: The famous Fifth Avenue Theatre offers Broadway fare in a stunningly resurrected space.

Right: A band entertains the crowd at Bumbershoot—Seattle's international music and arts festival, held every Labor Day weekend at the 74-acre Seattle Center.

Right: The glorious and arduous history of the Paramount Theatre started when Adolph Zukor opened it in the 1920's. Today Seattle Theatre Group welcomes Broadway plays, concerts, movies and more at the stunningly refurbished venue.

Famous in Seattle

Lots of local favorite sons and daughters

Above: Perhaps the best-known movie with Seattle in it's name

The world's most famous, wealthy, and philanthropic college dropout, one of the greatest rock guitarists who died young, the best-known glass artist of our era—these and many other famous folks hail from the Emerald City.

Bill Gates (William Henry Gates III) was born on October 28, 1955, to an upper middle class family. His mom, Mary, was community minded and encouraged civic engagement in her children. At prep school, where he met his friend and future partner Paul Allen, Bill got a stunning 1,590 out of 1,600 on his SATs, and subsequently entered Harvard in 1973. Bill left college a year later and the rest, as they say, is history.

Jimi (born Johnny Allen, but later changed to James Marshall) Hendrix was born here in 1942, and after a tumultuous youth, dropped out of high school, enlisted in the Army, and eventually started his music career as a session musician for Little Richard, Sam Cooke, and others.

Born in 1941 in Tacoma, Dale Chihuly discovered the possibilities of working with glass while studying interior design at the University of Washington. In 1968 he went to work at the famous Venini glass factory in Venice, Italy, and shortly thereafter returned to Washington to help found the Pilchuck Glass School. His glass art pieces are in more than 200 museums around the world.

These are just three of the world-renown Seattleites in a whole range of fields. In business we must remember Microsoft cofounder Paul Allen; Gordon Bowker, Jerry Baldwin, and Zev Siegel who founded Starbucks, and Howard

Left: The great Seattle rock legend, Jimi Hendrix

Below: Seattle's most prolific musical genius, Quincy Jones

Above: *Grey's Anatomy* takes place in the fictional Seattle Grace-Mercy Hospital.

Schultz who is its CEO. And, although he was born in Albuquerque, Jeff Bezos, the entrepreneur who gave us Amazon.com, has been at home in Seattle for a while.

Actors from Seattle include Carol Channing, Jeffrey Dean Morgan, Jean Smart, Rainn Wilson, Adam West, Frances Farmer, Brendan Fraser, Cameron Crowe, Josie Bissett, Ann Reinking, Brian Stokes Mitchell, Gypsy Rose Lee, and even Bruce Lee who lived here during high school.

Astronauts Richard F. Gordon Jr. and Stephen S. Oswald are both from Seattle, as are the writers Sherman Alexie and Terry Brooks.

Also included are musicians Ann and Nancy Wilson (Heart), Brandi Carlile, Judy Collins, Jennifer Warnes, Sir Mix-a-lot, Kenny G., Dave Matthews, Quincy Jones, Kurt Cobain, Dave Grohl, Nirvana, the Foo Fighters, Alice in Chains, Pearl Jam, Soundgarden, and the Gits.

Above: Kurt Cobain is often credited with being the father of the "grunge" movement with his band, Nirvana.

Right: Chuck Jones and one of his most beloved cartoon characters, the inimitable Bugs Bunny.

The list of beloved, infamous, and famous Seattleites is impressive. There is a batch of hit movies and television shows that feature the city, too. From *Sleepless in Seattle,* to *The Fabulous Baker Boys,* and *Say Anything* in cinema, and from *Fraser*

to *Grey's Anatomy* on TV, the images of the city have reached around the globe.

These brushes with fame are part of what make this city such a magnet for visitors from all over the world.

The Rise of Industry

A great place to work for brainy, college educated types

It started in 1910 when William Boeing bought the Heath shipyard on the Duwamish River in Seattle where he later built his first airplane factory. By 1915 Boeing had built a hangar next to Lake Union and a year later had crafted the B & W seaplane there. For the rest of the twentieth century, Boeing was a force to be reckoned with in aerospace, creating any number of planes, helicopters, and even rockets and space stations for commercial, government, and military uses—and employing thousands of Seattleites in the process. Due to mergers and changes in the company over time, there have been major layoffs in the Puget Sound aerospace giant starting in the 1980s and through the

Above: The earliest Boeing flies alongside the Dreamliner over Seattle.

Below: The world headquarters of Microsoft sprawls across several square miles in suburban Redmond, WA.

Left: Bill Gates, the wealthiest man in the world

1990s. Most recently, Boeing has moved its headquarters from Seattle to Chicago, leaving many workers without jobs.

Starting in the 1990s, however, Seattle became a hub for technologic innovation and industry. Microsoft, of course, is the giant in the area, with almost 41,000 local area employees, mostly at its Bellevue headquarters. But Microsoft is not the only tech-driven company in the Puget Sound. Other tech companies in the area include the web commerce behemoth, Amazon; game companies such as Nintendo, PopCap (recently purchased by Electronic Arts), BigFish (a casual game giant), Wizards of the Coast (creator of Dungeons and Dragons and Magic the Gathering). T-Mobile, the telecommunication giant, and Zillow, the online real estate powerhouse, are also major tech employers in the Seattle area.

Of course, there are more than a few other local businesses that have gone global: Starbucks and Nordstrom to name two.

Below: The corporate headquarters for the most famous coffee on earth.

Below: Big Fish Games is indeed a very big fish in the casual gaming world.

Art, Animals, Amps, and Guitars

Cultural institutions the Seattle way

Cultural experiences in major cities tend to have a lot in common: art museums and opera houses, the symphony, the zoo. Seattle has world-class examples in each of these areas too. But, not surprisingly, it has a few institutions you won't find anywhere else!

The Seattle Art Museum and its extension, the Olympic Sculpture Park, are mainstays of culture. First housed in the art deco building that is now occupied by the Seattle Asian Art Museum, SAM opened in 1933. In 1991 it opened in its new building, designed by internationally known architects Robert Venturi and Denise Scott Brown. In 2007 SAM added the impressive nine-acre sculpture park where visitors can view a wide range of outdoor art, as well as views of the Olympic Mountains and Puget Sound.

Seattle has a terrific Aquarium in Waterfront Park and a large zoo in Woodland

Above: Model of Yoda at the Science Fiction Museum

Left: The Museum of Flight is home to more than 85 aircraft.

Below: An alien monster exhibit is prepared at the Science Fiction Hall of Fame.

Above: The Experience Music Project and the Science Fiction Hall of Fame

Right: *Father and Son* by Louise Bourgeois graces a fountain in Olympic Sculpture Park.

Park. And science buffs will want to check out the Pacific Science Center in Seattle Center.

For history, there are museums like Wing Luke Museum of the Asian Pacific Experience, the Klondike Gold Rush National Historical Park, or even the Georgetown Power Plant Museum where visitors can witness the last operating examples of a large steam turbine. There is also the Museum of Flight, created to celebrate Boeing and its century of accomplishments in the area.

But if you are looking for something a bit more out of the box, there are several places to consider. At the Center for Wooden

Above: Experiencing the Seattle Art Museum starts with the stunning sculpture at its entrance.

Boats, encounter beautiful sailing craft old and new. At the Seattle Museum of Mysteries one can see exhibits about legends and lore of the Northwest, from Bigfoot to crop circles. And the most famous Seattle-only museum experience is the Experience Music Project. Created by Paul Allen and originally meant as a tribute only to Jimi Hendrix, the museum still has an impressive Hendrix collection. EMP was designed by legendary architect Frank Gehry and this controversial building is a must see, if only for the architecture and the Tower of Guitars at its entry. Surprisingly, the museum also houses the Science Fiction Museum and Hall of Fame.

Architecture and the Skyline

Buildings and structures new, old, rebuilt, and one of a kind

Right: This historic postcard shows a view of Seattle and the Puget Sound in the early 1900's.

Many cities have iconic skylines, and Seattle is certainly no exception. With the sweep of Puget Sound as a frame, the city rises, nestled into the hills beyond with the Space Needle and its restaurant twinkling against the night sky. The Needle famously started life as a sketch on a coffee shop placemat. The artist Edward E. Carlson was then the president of Western International Hotels. He was inspired by the Stuttgart Tower in Germany when he sketched his idea for the structure he hoped would be the center of the upcoming World's Fair. Not only would the finished Space Needle accomplish that, it would become an international symbol of Seattle itself for decades to come.

But the Space Needle is certainly not the only important work of architecture in the Emerald City. In the earliest days, Seattle was a collection of wooden frame buildings, but the great fire of 1889 destroyed most of them, and they were replaced by the brick and stone structures around the old part of town and Pioneer Square. The Pioneer Building, at the square, is one of the last great remaining Victorian buildings. In the early twentieth century art deco and beaux arts civic buildings rose on First and Beacon Hills, where some lovely examples remain.

The Arctic Building, on the corner of

Left: The waterfront and skyline make a spectacular vista.

Below: Downtown Seattle being rebuilt after the disastrous fire of 1890

3rd Avenue and Cherry Street in downtown Seattle, houses the Arctic Club. It was the first building in town to have a terra-cotta facade. These days it is most famous for the walrus heads with huge tusks that decorate that exterior.

In 1914 Smith Tower, near Pioneer Square, became the tallest building in the world outside of New York City. These days, the tallest building in the Pacific Northwest is the Columbia Center.

Contemporary architects are well represented in Seattle. From the Seattle Art Museum, designed by Venturi and Scott Brown, to Frank Gehry's undulating fusion of colors and textures—the Experience Music Project—there are a number of significant buildings in town. But none of these buildings has received the sort of international critical acclaim showered on the elegant Seattle Central Library designed by Rem Koolhas.

Below: These iconic walrus heads are the gargoyles that guard the Arctic Club.

Below: The beautiful Pioneer Building gives the Square its name.

Pioneer Square

A visitor's starting place

Above: A detail of the famous Tlingit Indian Totem pole

Covering 90 acres in the oldest part of town, Pioneer Square is a historic district with something for everyone. It's not really a square, though. It stretches between downtown proper in the north and the sports stadiums and the international district in the south. The area is famous for its cobblestone streets and horse-drawn carriages.

Notice the Tlingit Indian Totem pole? It first appeared in 1899 when it was stolen from the Alaskan tribe by Seattleites and erected here. In 1938, after vandals set it on fire, the pieces that were salvaged were sent back to the Tlingit people. Their craftsmen graciously created a reproduction of the totem pole as a gift for Seattle.

Just across the way from the totem pole is the Iron Pergola. This elaborate structure was built in 1909 as a cable car stop but today, after its restoration in the early 1970s it is a shady recreational space for visitors to the Pioneer Square area.

Below: The Alaska Ferry Terminal is a landmark of downtown Seattle.

Among the attractions located in Pioneer Square are the Seattle Art Museum, Benaroya Concert Hall, the Seattle Aquarium, and Waterfront Park. At the north end of the square is the famous Pike Place Market.

Within the square there are many restaurants, bars, coffee shops, and lots of antique shopping, and galleries. One favorite gallery is the Glasshouse Studio, where you can watch glassblowers create their art

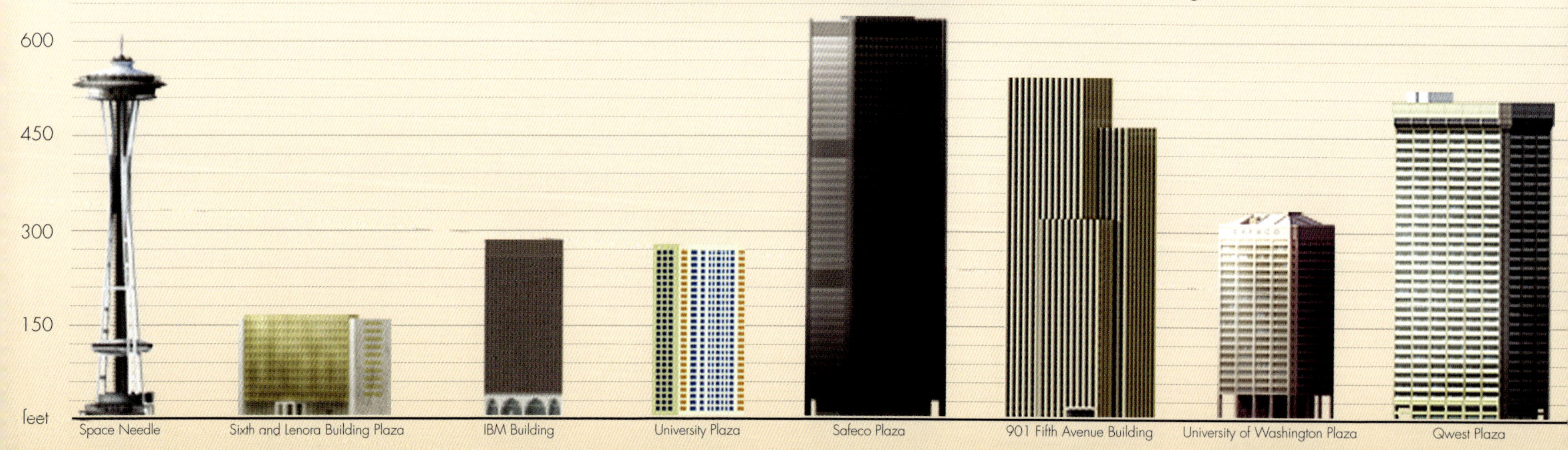

and buy a piece to take home, as well.

There are also a number of bookstores in Pioneer Square, including Seattle Mystery Bookshop, among others. And camping enthusiasts won't want to miss North Face, the best place for hiking, climbing, and camping equipment and clothing.

Right: Totem pole in Pioneer Square

Below: The Iron Pergola reminds visitors of the Metro in Paris, France.

Above: Customers browse through books at one of the numerous bookstores in Pioneer Square.

Pike Place Public Market

Watch those fish fly

Want to shop for books, artisanal cheese, Italian gourmet food, maps, gifts, a string of chili peppers, a bouquet of fresh flowers, a yummy treat, some local seafood, or veggies? Pike Place Market has all those and much more. It is the oldest continually operating public farmer's market in the U.S., making it the nation's "premier" farmer's market. It was rescued from urban renewal in 1971 to be named a historic district and has become a magnet for locals and visitors alike.

Left: At one of the great fish markets in the Pike Place Market, a fishmonger discusses the catch with patrons.

Below: Tourists and Seattleites alike contribute money in the charity "piggy bank" called Rachel who has pride of place at the market's entrance.

Starting outside, one can visit Rachel the Pig, a 550-pound bronze piggy bank created by artist Georgia Gerber, that turned 25 years old in 2011. Rachel has collected nearly $200,000 in every currency from visitors, which benefits the low-income and elderly residents of downtown Seattle.

In the North Arcade are kiosks and shops that all feature food and wares caught, grown, or made in the local area. From the world-famous fish throwers at Pike Place Fish Market to the Market Spice shop, the arcade is a crazy mixture of things to smell, taste, touch, hear, and buy!

Looking overhead, you may encounter a giant squid crafted in copper and nearby a

life-size wooden sculpture of Sasquatch, the legendary Northwestern Big Foot.

On the corner of the Economy Building is First and Pike News—an international news and magazine purveyor of magazines and papers from all corners of the globe. Inside, DeLaurenti's Specialty Food Market offers wines, cheeses, oils, and authentic Italian deli foods. While snacking at the market is tempting, visitors are wise to save room for one or more of the excellent dining options on offer. The Pink Door, World Class Chili, and Pike Pub & Brewery are just three of the fun places to eat in the market. And there are also international specialty restaurants, such as Mr. D's Greek Deli, Mee Sum Pastries, or Piroshky Piroshky.

There are even are three more levels below the market to explore. Down Under visitors find a wild mix of eclectic shops and stalls offering everything from supplies for a magic act to button and beads.

Below: Scanning the glorious fruits and veggies at the market is a mouthwatering pursuit.

Above: In its earlier days, delivery trucks unload merchandise at the market, circa 1912.

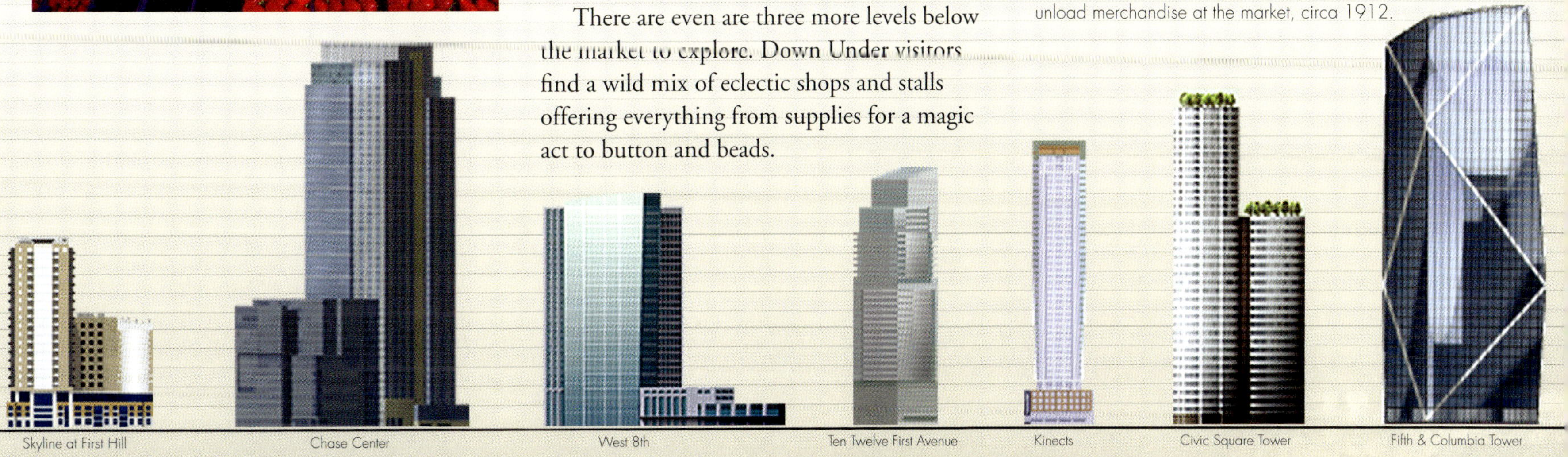

Play Ball

Sports and sport fans abound

Seattleites are active themselves and they also love their sports teams. Well, they love the teams that still play in Seattle, that is. The Emerald City got its first NBA team in 1966 and named it for the Boeing SST project: the Seattle SuperSonics. It became a team strong enough to compete in a few NBA finals and to win the title in 1979. But in 2006, after a failed attempt to motivate Washington State officials to fund a massive upgrade on Key Arena, the owners (led by Howard Schultz of Starbucks fame) sold the team to an Oklahoma businessman and it became known as the Oklahoma Thunder.

So who is playing in Key Arena now? The WNBA team the Storm was founded in 1999 and continues to play at the arena. The ladies have won two WNBA championships since: in 2004 and 2010.

As for football, Seattle boasts the Seahawks, an NFL team owned by Paul Allen (of Microsoft and Experience Music Project fame). Allen is also part owner of the Seattle Sounders soccer team and owner of the Portland Trailblazers of the NBA. The Seahawks have not won a Super Bowl, but have won division championships many years, including in 2010. Since 2002, the team plays at CenturyLink Field also known as Qwest Field or Seahawk Stadium.

Pro baseball in Seattle means the Mariners. An American League West team since 1977, the Mariners haven't won a World Series or a Pennant, but as recently as 2001, they won the ALW division championship. Since 1999 the team has played at Safeco Field.

And Seattle is home of great college teams, as well. The Washington State Cougars football team

Left: Qwest Field often sold out for Seahawks' games.

played in three bowl games in 2003, including the Rose Bowl. The Cougars basketball team has not won a championship since 1917.

University of Washington Huskies football has significant numbers of local fans. The university played its first football game in1889. Huskies basketball, however, is a powerhouse team, winning Pac-12 Championships in 2005, 2010, and 2011.

Right: The Kingdome comes down to make room for Qwest Field and the Seattle Mariner's baseball stadium, Safeco Field, shows off it's retractable roof. It's always good to be weather-proof in Seattle.

Below: The Seattle Seahawks play the New York Giants.

Below right: Ichiro Suzuki in action for the Seattle Mariners

Strange Seattle

Things you will only find here

Above: Where else could you watch sockeye salmon pass over a fish ladder on their way to spawn?

You'll find it in Fremont. If by "it" you mean a troll holding a Volkswagen beetle under a bridge—yes, under the Aurora Avenue Bridge is an 18-foot-high, climbable troll clutching an actual automobile and looking fierce. In 1989 the Fremont Arts Council commissioned this delightfully weird and beloved surprise. Also in the funky Fremont neighborhood are two other pieces of unexpected public art. A local bronze artist, who died before he could sell it for scrap, brought a statue of Vladimir Lenin back from Slovakia. It now resides near a brass foundry and has become a fixture of the district. Oh, and there's also the Fremont Rocket. Yes, it's an actual relic of the Cold War that rises atop a building a block away from Lenin.

One of the most peculiar sites in all of Seattle is the Gum Wall at the Pike Place Market. It's a wall where for quite a long time passersby have been leaving their ABC (already been chewed) gum. Now it has a following and whether one chooses to add to the facade or merely gape at it, the Gum Wall is certainly one of a kind.

Left: Care to add your chewed gum to this unique spot?

Right: Neon lights enhance the oddity of this surplus cold war rocket that stands as public art in Fremont.

Sightseers and locals alike may discover that they have met a spirit from beyond the grave while on The Market Ghost Tour at the Pike Place Market. Several of the ghosts that people claim continue to "live" in the market are so famous they have names: there's Frank, who appears at the Alibi Room restaurant,

and Jacob, who is said to have been a groom back in the days when the market had stables. Tours take an hour, and are offered Friday and Saturday evenings.

Salmon climb ladders in Seattle. They climb the Ballard Fish Ladder on the southern side of the Hiram M. Chittenden Locks. The fish ladder was constructed in 1976 to support the salmon as they fight their way to the spawning grounds in the Cascade headwaters of the Sammamish River.

Slightly less odd, but no less distinctly Seattle-ish, are two annual festivals. Seafair is a citywide festival with daily events that take place all over town during July and August. Races on land and sea, parades, a beauty pageant, and a pirate's landing are all typical experiences at Seafair. Bumbershoot is another uniquely Seattle affair. Started in 1971 as Festival '71, it drew the largest crowd to the Seattle Center since the World's Fair of 1962. It was three days of fun at the Center and it still is. Music of every kind, comedy, costumes, film, even a spelling bee all typify this Seattle-only event named for the most ubiquitous accessory in town—the umbrella.

Right: A flotilla of partiers convenes at Seafair to watch the Seafair Unlimited Hydroplane Races.

Below: Enter here for a spectral tour of history on Pike Place Market's Ghost Tour.

Right: The statue of Vladimir Lenin is installed in 1997.

Rainy Days

Brew the beans and the beer, grab a book and chill

If Napa and Sonoma are Wine Country, then Seattle must be Coffee Land. Seattle coffees are renowned the world over and an intrinsic part of the chilled-out Seattle lifestyle. The city that elevated coffee and coffee shops to their current abundance on street corners all over the world loves its java. There are unique and plentiful places to pop in for a cappuccino or latté all over town. Of course, Starbucks started it all, and the original Starbucks, opened in 1971 in Pike Place Market, is still serving up great coffees. But there are many more coffee shops in town. Monorail Espresso in downtown Seattle takes its name from the 1962 World's Fair transport. In Pioneer Square you will find Zeitgeist Coffee, opened in 1997, and voted best cup of coffee in 2000 by Seattle City Search. Here you will find a gigantic dictionary and a globe handy, should you need to settle an argument or expand your horizons. At Caffè Umbria, also in the Square, you can enjoy the coffee, but don't miss the gelato, too.

Other successful chains of coffee shops that started here include Tully's, Seattle's Best, and Peet's. But singular shops with local followings

Left: Rainier beer remains iconic of Seattle both here and around the world.

Below: Workers and horse drawn wagons outside the Rainier brewery in 1886

abound. They include Caffé Vita, Caffe Ladro Espresso Bar and Bakery, and Uptown Espresso. And if you just have to have a cup of tea instead, try the Crumpet Shop at the Pike Place Market for British charm.

There is one other drink that Seattleites appreciate to the point of becoming aficionados: locally brewed beer. It started with the first commercial brewery in 1854 and more than ten years before the city was founded, Rainier Beer was launched. More recently, Gordon Bowker, one of the founders of Starbucks, cofounded Seattle's Redhook Brewery in 1982.

Below: You can grab a cup of espresso at this drive through stand shown here parked in the lot of Spud Fish & Chips.

Microbrews and local brewpubs are all the rage in the Emerald City. There are many spots for a pint of local beer here. There is Big Time Brewery & Alehouse, Elysian Brewing Company, Hale's Ale Brewery & Pub, The Pike Brewing Company and Pub, Pyramid Alehouse, and on and on and on.

The other pastime that Seattleites are known for is reading. The well-educated and well-read population enjoys rainy afternoons lounging in and browsing the more than 150,000 volumes at Elliot Bay Book Company. The amazing literary purveyor occupies a building that was once the old Globe Building during the Gold Rush. It's worth a visit for the space, as well as the knowledge. Smaller, but equally popular local bookshops include Mystery Bookshop in Pioneer Square and, on Capitol Hill, Twice Sold Tales for used books.

Below: Pick up a cup of Peet's coffee or tea next to this unique architectural facade in the Fremont neighborhood.

Wish You Were Here

Views and memories of a special place

Your greetings from Seattle will surely be full of the adventures you had while exploring the city and beyond. Will you choose a classic image of the Space Needle twinkling in the sky above the city with the water sparkling beyond and the mountains that seem to embrace it all? Do you think a view of the Puget Sound from the ferry across is more emblematic of your experience? What about the flying fish at Pike Place Market? And the underground tours, or the Frank Gehry or Rem Koolhas buildings? You may need to use all the postcards you collect here and still want to add more for your own album. Seattle offers a surprisingly diverse and delightful array of experiences for visitors and locals alike. You adventured around town walking, hopping on a bus, grabbing the monorail or the streetcar, or maybe the water taxi or a ferry. Will your postcards home include images of these? Your memories of Seattle will remain bright, even if the weather was overcast and grey. That's just the sort of place this gem of the Northwest is.

Below and right: Its history may not be as long as Rome, or even New York, but images of the past show just how beautiful Seattle was and still is.

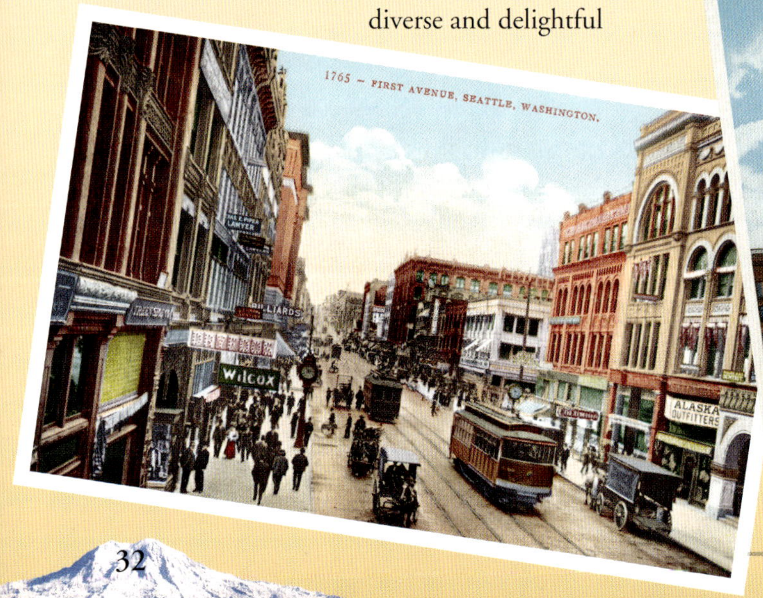

Seattle and Mount Rainier

POST CARD

PLACE
STAMP
HERE

Moon over the Space Needle, Seattle

POST CARD

PLACE
STAMP
HERE

Totem pole in Pioneer Square, Seattle

POST CARD

PLACE
STAMP
HERE

Downtown Seattle

POST CARD

PLACE
STAMP
HERE